AF292016

# About the Author

RUDOLF STEINER (1861–1925) called his spiritual philosophy 'anthroposophy', meaning 'wisdom of the human being'. As a highly developed seer, he based his work on direct knowledge and perception of spiritual dimensions. He initiated a modern and universal 'science of spirit', accessible to anyone willing to exercise clear and unprejudiced thinking.

From his spiritual investigations Steiner provided suggestions for the renewal of many activities, including education (both general and special), agriculture, medicine, economics, architecture, science, philosophy, religion and the arts. Today there are thousands of schools, clinics, farms and other organizations involved in practical work based on his principles. His many published works feature his research into the spiritual nature of the human being, the evolution of the world and humanity, and methods of personal development. Steiner wrote some 30 books and delivered over 6000 lectures across Europe. In 1924 he founded the General Anthroposophical Society, which today has branches throughout the world.

# INITIATIVE

*The karmic spiritual impulse of the followers of Michael*
*How Ahriman works into personal intelligence*

Lecture held in Dornach on 4 August 1924

## RUDOLF STEINER

Sophia Books

Sophia Books
An imprint of Rudolf Steiner Press
Hillside House, The Square
Forest Row RH18 5ES

www.rudolfsteinerpress.com

Published by Rudolf Steiner Press 2019

First published by Rudolf Steiner Press in *Karmic Relationships, Vol. III* in 1957. Translated by George Adams with revisions by D.S. Osmond. Revised for this edition by Matthew Barton

© Rudolf Steiner Press 2019

Originally published in German as part of the volume entitled *Esoterische Betrachtungen karmischer Zusammenhänge, Dritter Band* (volume 237 in the *Rudolf Steiner Gesamtausgabe* or Collected Works) by Rudolf Steiner Verlag, Dornach. This authorized translation is published by permission of the Rudolf Steiner Nachlassverwaltung, Dornach

All rights reserved. No part of this publication may be reproduced, stored in a retrieval system, or transmitted, in any form or by any means, electronic, mechanical, photocopying or otherwise, without the prior permission of the publishers

A catalogue record for this book is available from the British Library

ISBN 978 1 85584 564 0

Cover by Andrew Morgan featuring 'The Fall of the Rebel Angels' by Luca Giordano
Typeset by DP Photosetting, Neath, West Glamorgan
Printed and bound in Great Britain by 4Edge Limited, Essex

# Contents

# INITIATIVE

The fundamental feeling I have wanted to summon is this: In finding ourselves within the anthroposophical movement we should begin to feel something of the peculiar karmic position which the impulse to anthroposophy gives us. It must be recognized that in the ordinary course of life people feel very little of their karma. They confront life as though the experiences they acquire have happened by chance and fortuitous circumstance. They pay little heed to the fact that what we encounter in earthly life from birth to death contains inner, karmic relationships of destiny. And in the absence of any such thoughts, they may be all too prone to believe, for instance, in a kind of fatalism which calls human freedom into question.

I have often said that the more intensely we penetrate karmic connections, the more we discover the true essence of freedom. We need not fear, therefore, that by entering into the details of karmic relationships we shall lose our open and unimpaired vision of the essence of human freedom. I have described aspects connected with the former earthly lives, and lives between death and rebirth, of those who enter the Michael community. In every instance—and ultimately this relates to all of you—you will have seen the deep and significant part that spirit plays in the whole inner configuration of the soul.

In our materialistic age with all its circumstances, with its manner of education and upbringing, a person only sincerely embraces anthroposophy when he bears an inner karmic impulse that impels him toward the spirit. He will not otherwise truly embrace it. This karmic impulse contains the sum of all the experiences which he underwent in the way I have described, before he came down into his present earthly life.

Now, my dear friends, when a person is thus strongly united with spiritual impulses that work directly upon his soul, he will, as he descends from the spiritual into the physical world, enter less deeply, unite himself less strongly with his external, bodily nature. All those who have grown into the Michael stream as above described, were thus predestined to enter into this physical body with a certain reserve, if I may put it like that. This, too, lies deep in the karma of the souls of anthroposophists.

On the other hand, we will always find that those whose inner impulse is quite consciously and anxiously to hold themselves at a distance from things anthroposophical, are fully and firmly established in their physical bodily nature. In the people of today who embrace the spiritual life which anthroposophy seeks to give, we find a looser relationship, at any rate, between the astral body and I-organization on the one hand, and the physical and etheric organization on the other.

Now this means that such a person will less easily come to terms with his life. He will find life less easy to deal with, for the simple reason that he has more possibilities to choose from than other people, because he easily grows away from what others grow into. Think only, my dear friends, to what an intense degree many people today *are* what the connections of outer life have made of them. No one can doubt that they suit these connections, however odd this may sometimes seem. Look at a clerk, a business person, a builder, a contractor, a factory owner, and so forth. They are what they are in an absolutely self-evident way. There is no question about it. True, such a person will sometimes say he feels he was born for a better, or at any rate a different kind of life; but he does not mean it very seriously. And now compare with this the infinite difficulties we find in those who are drawn by an inner impulse into the spiritual life of anthroposophy. Perhaps we see it nowhere with such remarkable intensity as in the young, and notably the youngest of the young.

Take for instance the older pupils of the Waldorf School, those in the higher classes of the school. We find, both in our boys and girls, that they progress comparatively quickly in their soul-spiritual development. But this does not make life any easier to take hold of for these young people. On the contrary, it generally becomes more difficult—far more complicated. The possibilities become broader and more far-reaching. In the ordinary course of modern life (with certain exceptions), it is not too difficult for teachers of adolescents to find the ways and means of giving their pupils sound advice. But when we bring on our children as we do in the Waldorf School, it becomes far more difficult to give advice, for the simple reason that universal humanity is more developed in them. The wide horizon which a boy or girl acquires in the Waldorf

School places before their inner vision a greater range and scope of possibilities.

It is essential, therefore, that Waldorf teachers—who have been guided to this calling by their karma—acquire a wide horizon and a broad outlook, a knowledge of the world and a sound feeling of what is going on in the world. In this respect all the details of educational method are far less important than having a broad outlook. Here again, in the karma of such a teacher, we see how large the number of possibilities become; far, far greater than in ordinary life. The child or adolescent presents the Waldorf teacher, in turn, not with specific, but with manifold and many-sided riddles.

The real karmic conditions and pre-disposing causes of all that impels people to anthroposophy will best be understood if we speak not in pedantic definition, but rather hint at these things in one way or another, by characterizing the atmosphere in which, if I may put it like this, anthroposophists express and unfold their lives.

All this makes it necessary for the anthroposophist to pay heed to *one* condition of his karma, a condition that is sure to be present in him to a high degree. Much can be said—and we shall still have much to say—about why one or another character or temperament is drawn to anthroposophy in consequence of what has happed in the spiritual world, as I described. But all these impulses, which bring individual anthroposophists to anthroposophy, have as it were a counterpart, which the spirit of the world has made stronger in them than in other people. All these many possibilities existing in regard to the most manifold things in life demand *initiative* from the anthroposophist—*inner initiative*. We must become aware of this.

The anthroposophist must apply the following principle to himself. He must say this: Now that I have become an anthroposophist through my karma, the impulses which have drawn me to anthroposophy require me to be attentive and alert. For somehow or somewhere, more or less deeply in my soul, there will emerge the need for me to find *inner initiative* in life—initiative of soul which will enable me to undertake something or to make some judgment or decision out of my own inmost being. Truly, in the karma of every anthroposophist is inscribed this exhortation: *Be a person of initiative, and take care that the hindrances of your own body, or hindrances that otherwise confront you, do not prevent you from finding the centre of your being, where the source of your initiative lies. Likewise you will find that all joy and sorrow, all happiness and pain, depend on finding or not finding your own individual initiative.* This should stand continually, inscribed as in golden letters, before the soul of the anthroposophist. Initiative lies in his karma, and much of what meets him in this life will depend on the extent to which he can become willingly, actively conscious of it.

You must realize that these few words contain something hugely important. For in our time so many things can lead people astray in terms of all that guides and directs their judgment; and without clear appraisal of circumstances and conditions, initiative will not find the way to emerge from the soul's deep foundations.

Now, what is it that can bring us to clear judgment about life, especially in these times? My dear friends, let us here consider one of the most important and characteristic features of our age and, in relation to it, try to find out how we can develop a certain clarity of judgment. In what I am now going to say we have, as you will see, a kind of 'egg of Columbus'. In this story of the egg of Columbus, the challenge was to discover how to stand the egg up on its end without it falling over. In what I shall now discuss, a similarly insightful solution is required.

We live in the age of materialism. All that is destined to occur around and within us is governed by materialism on the one hand, and on the other by the intellectualism that is now so widespread. I characterized this intellectualism yesterday when I spoke of journalism and of the impulse everywhere to discourse on world affairs in public meetings, mass meetings and the like. We must recognize the extent to which people today are subject to the influences of these two contemporary currents. For it is almost as impossible to escape from these two, from intellectualism and materialism, as it is to avoid getting wet if you go out in the rain without an umbrella. These things are around us everywhere. After all, there are certain things we simply cannot know (and yet we have to know), which we cannot know unless we read them in the papers. There are certain things we cannot learn (and we *have* to learn them) unless we learn them as materialism dictates. How can anyone become a doctor today unless they are willing to consume a good portion of materialism? They have to imbibe this materialism as a self-evident matter, and if they are unwilling to do so, they cannot qualify as a physician in the modern sense. Thus we are perpetually exposed to these things. But this also plays very strongly into our karma.

But all this is perfectly suited to undermining initiative in human souls. Every public meeting, every large assembly to which people go, only fulfils its purpose as such if it undermines the initiative of the individuals involved, with the exception of the speakers and leaders. Nor does any newspaper fulfil its purpose if it does not create an atmosphere of opinion, thus again undermining individual initiative.

These things must be recognized. Moreover, we must remember that ordinary human consciousness is a very tiny chamber in the soul, while all that is going on around us, in the forms which I have just described, has a gigantic influence on our subconscious life. And after all, we have no alternative. Beside the fact that we are human beings pure and simple, we must be 'contemporaries' of our age. Some people think it is possible in any era to be 'purely' human, but this too would be disastrous, for we must also be men and women of our era. Of course it is bad if we are no more than this; but we *must* be contemporaries of our age, that is to say, we must have a feeling of what is going on in our own time.

Now it is true that many anthroposophists allow themselves to be sundered from a living feeling of present conditions, preferring to burble about a timeless sphere. In this respect one has the strangest experiences in conversation with anthroposophists. They may well know, for instance, who Lycurgus was, but display a naïve ignorance of their contemporaries.

This is because such a person—pre-disposed as he is to the unfolding of inner initiative—possesses a quality by virtue of his karma that (forgive the comparison) is like a bee which has a sting but is afraid to use it at the right moment. The sting is the initiative, but the person is afraid to use it. He is afraid, above all, of stinging into the ahrimanic realm. It is not that he is afraid of hurting this ahrimanic domain but that he fears the sting will recoil upon himself. This, to some extent, is what his fear is like. Thus, through an indeterminate fear of life, his initiative remains inactive.

These are the things which we must recognize. Encountering materialism everywhere, in theory and practice, our initiative is impeded. If anthroposophists have a sense for these things, they will perceive how their deepest impulses of will are derailed or foiled by theoretical and practical materialism. But this shapes karma in a strange way. If you observe yourselves truly, you will discover something of it in your lives each day, from morning to evening. And this naturally gives rise to a general desire to prove, theoretically and practically, the falsehood of materialism. This impulse lives in the hearts and minds of many anthroposophists. Somehow or other they want to demonstrate the falsehood of materialism. This is the enigma, the riddle that life has set so many of us in theory and practice:

How shall we contrive to prove the falsehood of materialism?

There are highly educated and learned people—you will find many such people in the Anthroposophical Society—who, when they have woken up to anthroposophy, feel a tremendous impulse to refute materialism, to fight it, to say all manner of things against it. So they begin to attack and refute materialism, maybe thinking that by doing so they stand fully within the stream of Michael. But as a rule they meet with little success. And it has to be acknowledged that such things said against materialism, though often founded on very good will, do not succeed. They make no impression on either the theory or practice of materialism. Why is this?

This is the very thing that hinders our clarity of judgment. Here stands the anthroposophist. To avoid his initiative being hampered, he wants to be clear what it is that confronts him in materialism. He wants to probe the wrongness of materialism to its foundations. But as a rule he finds little success. He thinks he is refuting materialism, but it continually rises again. Why is this so?

Now the egg of Columbus comes into its own. Why is this state of affairs so, my dear friends? It is due to the simple fact that materialism is true. I have said this many times. Materialism is not wrong, it is quite right. Here lies the reason. And the anthroposophist should learn, albeit in a very particular way, that materialism is right. He should learn it in this way: materialism is right, but it applies only to the outer physical body. The others, who are materialists, know only the physical realm, or at least they think they know it. The error lies here, not in materialism itself. When we learn anatomy or physiology or matters of practical life in the materialistic way, we learn the truth, but it holds good in the physical realm alone. Out of the inmost depths of our being we must profess the truth that materialism is right *in its own domain*—and indeed that it is the splendid achievement of our era to have discovered what is right and true in the realm of materialism. But this also has its practical, its karmically practical aspect.

It can be the karma of an anthroposophist to feel the following: I live with human beings with whom karma has united me. (I spoke of this yesterday.) Here I am, living with human beings who only subscribe to materialism. They only know what is true of physical life, and they cannot approach anthroposophy because they are misled by the very correctness of the knowledge that they possess.

Now, my dear friends, we live in the age of Michael, and in our souls is the intellectuality that lapsed from Michael. When Michael himself administered cosmic intelligence, these things were different. Then, cosmic intelligence continually tore the soul free from what existed as materialism. There were of course materialists even in former ages, but not as in our time. In former ages a person might be a materialist.

Then, I and astral body were implanted in his physical and etheric body. He felt his physical body. But the cosmic intelligence that Michael administered tore his soul free from it time and again. Today we are side by side—indeed we are often karmically united—with people in whom things are as follows: They too have the physical body, but the cosmic intelligence has now fallen away from Michael, has lapsed from him, and lives individually—personally, as it were—in the human being. Hence the I—all that is soul and spirit—remains in the physical body. Thus there are, standing alongside us, people whose soul and spirit has become deeply submerged in their physical body.

This is the truth we must acknowledge as we live alongside non-spiritual human beings. And inevitably this does not only call forth in us sympathy or antipathy in the ordinary sense, but is an experience that can indeed be a shattering one, my dear friends. To realize how tragic, how deeply moving an experience it must be, to live thus side-by-side with materialists (who, as I said before, are right in their own way), we need only look at those among them who are often highly gifted and who, out of certain instincts, may have very good impulses indeed; yet they cannot come to spirituality.

We see the tragedy of it when we come to consider the great gifts and noble qualities of many of those who are materialists. For after all, it is beyond question that those who, in this decisive time, do not find their way to the spirit, will suffer harm in their soul-life in their next incarnation. Great as their qualities may be, they will suffer harm. And when we see and recognize how, through their karma, a number of human beings today have the inner impulse to spirituality while others cannot approach it, our karmic connection with them should elicit a deep response within our souls. It should touch us and move us with a sense of tragedy. Until it does so, we shall never come to terms with our own karma. For if we sum up all that I have said of Michaelism (if I may now so call it), then we shall find this: the Michaelites are indeed inwardly imbued by a power that seeks to work from the spiritual realm into the whole human being, right down to the physical.

I described it yesterday as follows: these human beings are casting aside the element of race—the element whereby natural existence gives the human being such or such [an outward] stamp. If a person is imbued by the spirit in this earthly incarnation by virtue of becoming an anthroposophist, this prepares him to become in future someone no longer distinguished so much by external features but rather by what he was in this present incarnation. Let us be conscious of this in all humility. The time will come when the spirit will reveal in such human beings its own power to form the physiognomy—to shape the whole human form.

In the whole previous history of the world, such a thing has never yet occurred before. Hitherto, human physiognomies have arisen and emerged from nationality, from physical attributes. Today we can still tell from human faces, where they hail from—especially when they are young, when the cares of life or the joys and divine enthusiasms of life have not yet left their mark. But in times to come, there will be human beings whose physiognomy and features alone will reveal what they were in their past incarnation. It will be apparent that in their past incarnation they worked their way through to spiritual things. Then, standing and living beside others, what will karma signify? Karma will then have shed its otherwise customary affinities.

My dear friends, in this respect someone who takes life in real earnest will tell you this: one has been karmically united, or is still karmically united, with many who cannot find their way into spirituality. And however much kinship may still be left in life, a more or less deep estrangement, a justified estrangement will make itself felt. The karmic connections that would otherwise ordinarily work themselves out in life, fall away; they fade. But something different remains. I would put it like this: nothing remains of karma between one who stands within materialism and one who stands within spirituality—except for this: that the former must see and perceive the latter, and will become attentive to him. We can look to a future when those who in the course of the twentieth century increasingly approach things of the spirit, will stand side by side with others who were karmically united with them in a former life on earth. In that future time, karmic affinities, karmic relationships, will make themselves felt far less. But of karmic relationships this will have remained: those who stand within materialism will inevitably see and witness those who stand within spirituality. Those who were materialists today will in the future have to look continually upon those who embraced spirituality. This will be the karmic remnant.

Once again a shattering, a deeply moving fact, my dear friends. And to what end? Truly it lies in a far-reaching, divine cosmic plan. For how do modern materialists allow anything to be proven to them? By having it before their eyes—by being able to touch it with their hands. Those who subscribe to materialism will be able to see with their eyes and touch with their hands those with whom they once were karmically united, perceiving in their physiognomy, in their whole expression, what the spirit really is, for it will have become creative in outer form and feature. In such human beings it will thus be proven, visibly to human eyes, that the spirit is a creative power in the world. And it will be part of the karma of anthroposophists to demonstrate, for those who today embrace materialism, that the spirit truly exists, and testifies to itself in human beings themselves through the wise resolves of the gods.

But to arrive at this point, it will be necessary for us to confront intellectualism, not in a vague and nebulous way, but truly. We must not go out, my dear friends, without an umbrella. By this I mean that we are exposed to all I described above as the two streams—all the journalism, all the talk in public meetings. In the same way we cannot avoid getting wet if we go out without an umbrella, so these things too are unavoidable. At this tender and impressionable age—between 20 and 24—we have to pursue our studies (whatever they may be) through materialistic books. Yes, at this impressionable age it is unavoidable that in our studies we are imbued with and prepared for materialism. As we study what we have to, we are being schooled in materialism by the very structure and configuration of the language used, the very form of sentences. However we defend ourselves against it, we are nevertheless being prepared for materialistic outlooks.

Such a thing cannot be countered by merely formal arguments. We cannot shield a person today from this exposure to intellectual materialism. To write non-materialistic text-books on botany or anatomy today, simply would not suffice. Actual circumstances will not permit of it. The point, my dear friends, is that we should take hold of these things in no merely formal sense but in their reality. We must understand that since Michael no longer draws the soul and spirit forth from our physical bodily nature as in times past, Ahriman can do as he wills with the soul and spirit as it lives within the body. Above all, when the spirit–soul is highly gifted and is yet deeply immersed in the body, then, especially, it can be exposed to Ahriman. Ahriman finds his prey precisely in the most gifted of people, in order to sunder the intelligence from Michael, distance it from Michael.

Here especially, something occurs which plays a far greater part in our time than is generally thought. The ahrimanic spirits, though they cannot incarnate, can incorporate themselves; temporarily, they can penetrate human souls, permeate human bodies. In such moments the brilliant and overpowering spirit of an ahrimanic intelligence is stronger than anything that an individual person possesses—far, far stronger. Then, however intelligent he may be, however much he may have learned, and especially if his physical body is thoroughly pervaded by all his learning, an ahrimanic spirit can for a time incorporate itself in him. Then it is Ahriman who looks out of his eyes, Ahriman who moves his fingers, Ahriman who blows his nose, Ahriman who walks.

Anthroposophists must not recoil from knowledge such as this. For such a thing alone can bring the realities of intellectualism before our souls. Ahriman is a great and outstanding intelligence, and Ahriman's purpose with earthly evolution is overwhelming and thorough. He makes use of every opportunity where the spiritual aspect has become so strongly, bodily incorporated in someone, when the spirit takes such strong hold on the body, that consciousness is thereby in a sense dimmed or impaired. Ahriman seizes this opportunity. And then it happens (for in our era this has become possible) that a brilliant spirit takes possession of the human being, overpowering the human personality; and such a spirit, dwelling within a human personality and overpowering him, is able to work upon earth—able to work just like a human being.

This is the immediate endeavour of Ahriman, and it is strong. I have told you about the reappearance at the end of this century of those who now come to the things of the spirit and take them in full earnestness and sincerity.[*] But this is also the time, above all, that ahrimanic spirits will seek to use most strongly. Their hour will come then because human beings are so completely enmeshed in the intelligence that has overcome them and have become so unbelievably clever.

We are already quite nervous today when we encounter a very clever person, and can scarcely

---

[*] See e.g. lecture of 18 July 1924 in *Karma of Anthroposophy*, Rudolf Steiner Press 2009.

ever escape from such anxiety, for almost all are clever. Really, we cannot avoid this anxiety about human cleverness. And it is true to say that the cleverness being cultivated in this way is employed by Ahriman. And once human bodies are especially fit for this dimming or dulling of consciousness, it may happen that Ahriman himself appears, incorporated in human form.[*] Twice already, as can be demonstrated, Ahriman himself has appeared as an author. And for those anthroposophists who seek a clear and true vision of life, in this case too it will be vital not to be misled.

For what is the use, my dear friends, of someone publishing a book under his name when he is not really the author? The true author is then confused with another. And if Ahriman is the author of a book, nothing good can come of it if we think the author is a human being,

---

[*] See also *The Incarnation of Ahriman*, Rudolf Steiner Press 2006.

unless we perceive who the true author is. For, with his brilliant gifts, Ahriman can find his way into everything—he can slip into the very style of a human writer. What good can come of it if Ahriman is the real author, and we mistake it for a human work? To acquire the power of discrimination in this sphere, too, is absolutely necessary, my dear friends.

I wanted to make this point, in general describing a phenomenon which is playing its part in our present era. In next Friday's lecture I shall speak of such phenomena in greater detail.[*]

---

[*] This would be the lecture of 8 August 1924. See *Karmic Relationships*, Vol. III, Rudolf Steiner Press 1977.

# Further Reading

**Rudolf Steiner's fundamental books:**

*Knowledge of the Higher Worlds*
also published as: *How to Know Higher Worlds*

*Occult Science*
also published as: *An Outline of Esoteric Science*

*Theosophy*

*The Philosophy of Freedom*
also published as: *Intuitive Thinking as a
Spiritual Path*

**Some relevant volumes of Rudolf Steiner's lectures:**

*The Incarnation of Ahriman*
*The Karma of Anthroposophy*
*Karmic Relationships, Vol. III*
*Manifestations of Karma*

**Other budget-priced volumes from
Rudolf Steiner Press:**

*Single lectures:*
The Dead Are With Us
Educating Children Today
An Exercise for Karmic Insight
The Four Temperaments
How Can I Find the Christ?
How to Cure Nervousness
The Second Coming of Christ
The Work of the Angel in Our Astral Body

*Meditations:*
Calendar of the Soul, The Year Participated
The Foundation Stone Meditation
Meditations for Courage and Tranquility
Meditations for Harmony and Healing
Meditations for the Dead
Meditations for Times of Day and Seasons of
the Year

For all titles contact Rudolf Steiner Press (UK) or
SteinerBooks (USA): www.rudolfsteinerpress.com
www.steinerbooks.org